A Guide to Navigating Childhood Development and Wellbeing

Revised Edition

Dr. Niru Prasad

A Guide to Navigating Childhood Development and Wellbeing
Revised Edition
Copyright © 2022 by Dr. Niru Prasad

All rights reserved. No part of this publication may be reproduced, distributed, or transmitted in any form or by any means, including photocopying, recording, or other electronic or mechanical methods, without the prior written permission of the publisher or author, except in the case of brief quotations embodied in critical reviews and certain other noncommercial uses permitted by copyright law.

Although every precaution has been taken to verify the accuracy of the information contained herein, the author and publisher assume no responsibility for any errors or omissions. No liability is assumed for damages that may result from the use of information contained within.

Library of Congress Control Number:		2022910092
ISBN-13:	Paperback:	978-1-64749-769-9
	ePub:	978-1-64749-770-5

Printed in the United States of America

GoToPublish LLC
1-888-337-1724
www.gotopublish.com
info@gotopublish.com

FOREWORD

Dr. Niru Prasad has been a practicing pediatrician for over 40 years, specializing in emergency medicine and clinical practice with the Henry Ford Hospital in Detroit, Michigan. She has conducted extensive research into preventative health models for children and parents, with a focus on providing support for the childhood developmental process. Dr. Prasad has received several awards for her research and practice as a pediatrician, most notably the National Medal of Medicine, the Claude Pepper Certificate of Merit, and the Blue Cross Blue Shield Angel Caring Award. She now practices advisory medicine part-time, and enjoys spending time with her four children and eight grandchildren, aged 2 to 21.

PREFACE

This book serves as a personal culmination of over 50 years in the medical profession. For my entire career, I have been most motivated by issues of pediatrics, and thus the majority of my research, treatment patterns, and expertise has been surrounding the clinical aspects of pediatric medicine.

Beginning in the late 1990s, the American medical community increasingly began emphasizing the importance of the social aspects of upbringing as health determinants. For the first time, a child's socioeconomic status, mental state, genetic background, parental upbringing, sleep patterns, and many other non-pathological or pathology-adjacent characteristics were medicalized to the same extent as, for example, the last time a child was exposed to influenza, or which immunizations they had. Pediatricians across the country began to look for health risks that were not immediately "heath-related" at first glance. Over time, it has become clear that this holistic, comprehensive approach to pediatrics is far superior to preceding models.

As the pediatric academic landscape has changed, so too have its doctors. I have taken great care to assimilate the conclusions of leading scientists and industry practices from the last few decades into my everyday practice, which has lead to improving the lives of all my patients.

Many of my colleagues have also changed the way in which they perceive medicine—indeed, the contemporary hospital-driven push towards holistic, personalized medicine is reflective of a decades-long shift in commercial, personal, and social perception of what "health" even means.

This book contains a variety of longitudinal health strategies, experiences, and suggestions for parents on how to nurture and raise a child in today's American health climate. Perhaps most importantly, I have synthesized the social approach to healthcare with a robust and rigorous tradition of pathology-focused clinical care. By utilizing these distinct yet interdependent approaches in tandem, one is able to most effectively, successfully, and lovingly attend to the health needs of a child in today's day and age— a more mindful approach to parenting.

I am both humbled and excited to share my experiences with you. Thank you for reading my suggestions, and I wish to both you and your family a healthy and happy life.

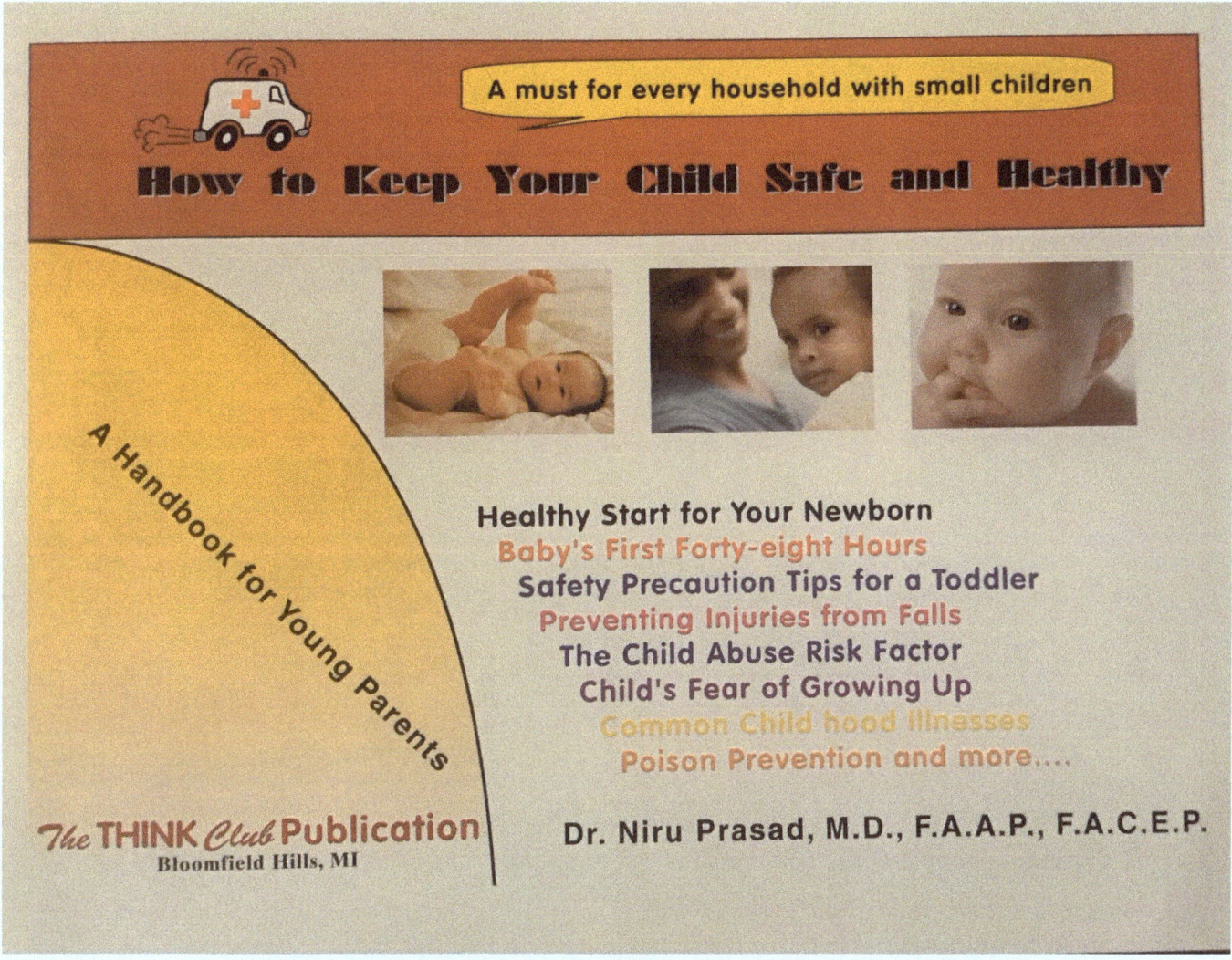

Dr. Prasad's first book on pediatrics in the modern age.

CHAPTER 1

Preschool Development

SECTION 1
Recommended Nutrition and Eating Habits

> **Summary**
> 1. Carefully curate the snacks and meals your child eats at home and at school
> 2. Work with a dietician to properly space out meals to match your child's metabolism
> 3. Set a good example by following nutritional guidelines from ChooseMyPlate.Gov

Preschool years are a time for significant rapid brain and cognitive development.

Preschoolers are beginning to transition from being fed by parents to a desire to self-select their foods. How advanced they may be depends on their temperament and linguistic abilities.

A major concern for many parents is ensuring their pre-school age children have proper nutrition. This age group needs to eat adequate amounts of fruits, vegetables, grains, proteins, and dairy and fortified soy alternatives. How much they consume during a typical day depends on their age, sex, and level of physical activity, but it should be in the range of 1200-1600 calories/day. Every child is different with varying growth patterns. Your pediatrician will have growth charts that follow your child's maturity and any concerns should be addressed with the doctor. Calorie counting is not needed for this age as it is more important to instill good habits and offer a variety of foods.

Select meals and snacks with limited sugars, sodium, and saturated fats. Establishing healthy habits at a young age is essential for development and prevention of various health conditions later in life, such as high blood pressure, heart disease, or diabetes. In addition, a healthy diet has been linked with better performance in school, increased cognitive functions, improved mood, and a stronger memory.

By the time they get to preschool, kids should be able to feed themselves and be eating a variety of foods from all these food groups: meat, dairy, fruits, vegetables, grains—and with different colors and textures they will be more likely to eat it willingly.

Childhood obesity rates have tripled over the last thirty years and children have increasing become one of the largest groups to consume ultraprocessed foods. Long-term obesity can yield much harm to the human body including high cholesterol and triglyceride levels, increased risk of cardiovascular disease, diabetes, certain cancers, and other social and psychological concerns.

While the current evidence is limited but evolving, it shows that certain factors in a school environment can positively influence the health of students and improve academic achievement. For parents, knowing the evidence is important to help make the case for addressing healthy eating and physical activity in schools, and at home.

For example, skipping breakfast is associated with decreased cognitive performance (e.g., alertness, attention, memory, processing of complex visual display, problem solving) among students, while a lack of adequate consumption of specific foods, such as fruits, vegetables, or dairy products, is associated with lower grades. Scientific studies are ongoing in search of potential links between refined sugars and aspartame as possible causes of hyperactivity, attention deficit, and behavioral problems in children. Deficits of specific nutrients (i.e., vitamins A, B6, B12, C, folate, iron, zinc, and calcium), and prolonged periods of hunger are also associated with lower grades and also higher rates of absenteeism and tardiness. The graphics provide examples of foods that provide such nutrients and some can be eaten on the go as easy snacks.

Learning what to eat is important, but so is understanding when and how much to consume. Establishing these habits early will serve children well their whole lives. During preschool years parents can teach kids about nutrition and making healthy choices which will set them up for their next step to kindergarten. For picky eaters, it may take numerous times for them to learn to accept that food.

Proper timing goes hand in hand with a proper diet. Family mealtimes eaten at regular intervals can also be used to encourage table manners, and improve conversation. Parents can use this time to make healthy choices for themselves since impressionable young children mimic what their parents do. Skip the fried foods and select the same thing that you would like them to eat. Some healthy substitutes for common household foods that your child may enjoy include:

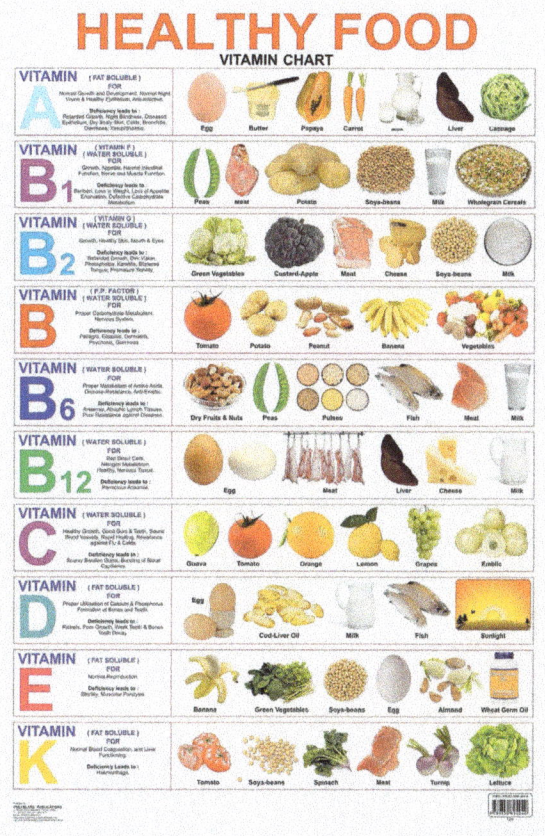

- Preservative free fruit bites (gummy fruit snacks)
- Lentil or home made chips (potato or tortilla chips)
- Grain bars (granola)
- Mashed potatoes made with reduced-fat milk (french fries)
- Oven fried chicken (fried chicken/frozen nuggets)
- Tube yogurt or frozen greek yogurt (ice cream)

- Reduced-fat cheddar (regular cheese)

The next page includes a commonly used example of what a child's typical plate should look like, broken down by nutritional food group. This graphic, provided by the Department of Agriculture, is commonly used by pediatricians and schools. Familiarity with this graphic will help you set up the right quantities of the food groups for your child. Remember to reward your child with attention and hugs, instead of candy and junk food.

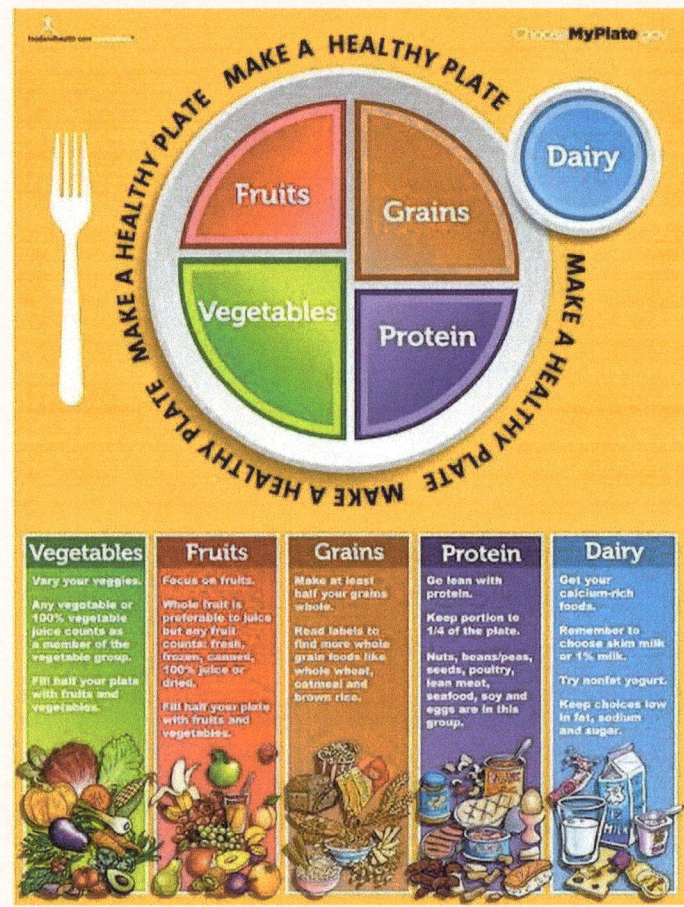

https://www.myplate.gov/

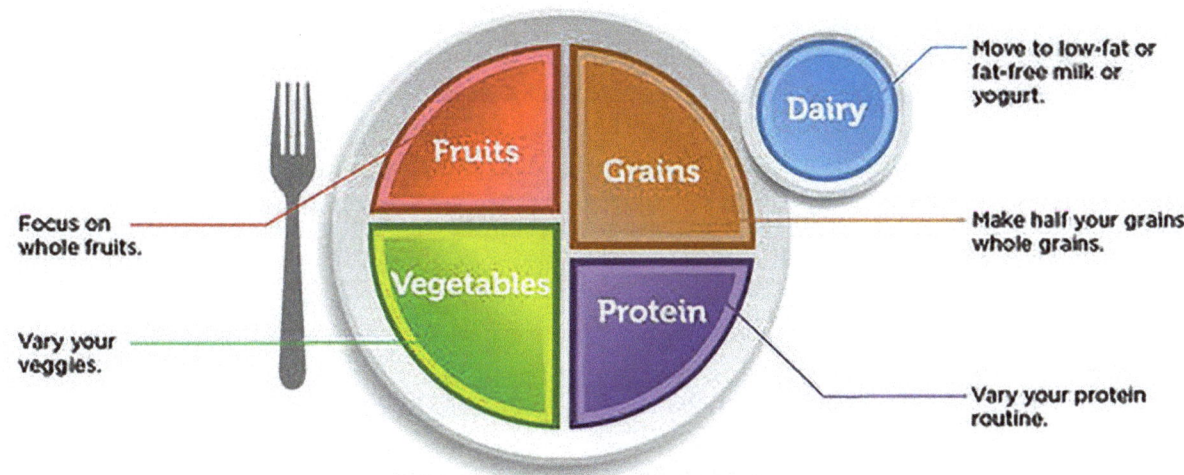

SECTION 2
Immunizations and Wellness

> **SUMMARY**
> 1. Stay up to date with your child's school on the required vaccinations
> 2. Monitor for post-injection symptoms such as soreness or a rash
> 3. Consult a pediatrician with worries or questions

Immunization as defined by the CDC is: "A process by which a person becomes protected against a disease through vaccination. This term is often used interchangeably with vaccination or inoculation." Vaccination is the act in the body to create immunity to a certain disease. This is done by using small amounts of a killed or weakened germ that causes the disease. Germs can be viruses (such as measles) or bacteria (such as pneumococcus). Vaccines stimulate the immune system to react as if there were a real infection. It fends off the "infection" and remembers the germ. Then, it can fight the germ if it enters the body later.

Immunizations are one of the best means of protection against contagious diseases. Vaccines have protected us from some of the following diseases: varicella/chicken pox, diphtheria, hepatitis A and B, HPV, measles, Hib, and meningococcal, mumps, polio, rotavirus, rubella, pertussis/

whooping cough, tetanus, pneumococcal, etc. Many of these diseases can cause serious complications and even kill the person.

Healthy children have better attendance patterns and do better academically. Most schools require proof of immunizations before children will be allowed to attend school. Vision and dental examinations are also required at different grade levels but those vary by state. Health insurance can provide students and their families with comprehensive health care coverage for doctor visits, immunizations, medications, and eye and dental exams.

Knowing what vaccinations your child will need for school, and to stay safe when traveling can be a confusing process. Staying on track with these vaccine schedules will require regular appointments with your child's pediatrician. The doctors keep a record of the shots so if you move or change pediatricians be sure to take a copy of those records with you.

Vaccines are generally broken down into four different categories:

- Attenuated (weakened) live viruses are used in some vaccines such as in the measles, mumps, and rubella (MMR) vaccine.
- Killed (inactivated) viruses or bacteria are used in some vaccines, such as in IPV.
- Toxoid vaccines contain an inactivated toxin produced by the bacterium. For example, the diphtheria and tetanus vaccines are toxoid vaccines.
- Conjugate vaccines (such as Hib) contain parts of bacteria combined with proteins.

So what vaccinations does your child need?

The following vaccinations are recommended by

- diphtheria and tetanus vaccines are toxoid vaccines.
- Conjugate vaccines (such as Hib) contain parts of bacteria combined with proteins.

So what vaccinations does your child need?

The following vaccinations and schedules are set by the Centers for Disease Control and Prevention (CDC). Some variations are normal, and recommendations change as new vaccines are developed. Your doctor will talk to you about the right vaccinations and schedule for your child.

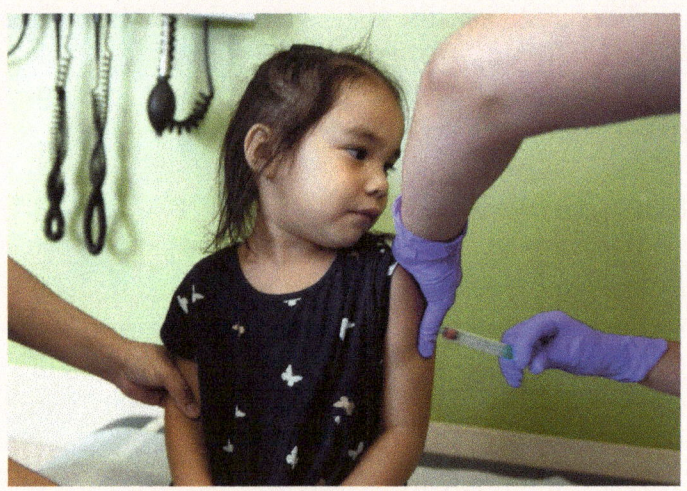

Recommended vaccinations:

- Chickenpox (varicella) vaccine
- Diphtheria, tetanus, and pertussis vaccine (DTaP)
- Hepatitis A vaccine (HepA)
- Hepatitis B vaccine (HepB)
- Hib vaccine
- Human papillomavirus (HPV) vaccine
- Influenza vaccine
- Measles, mumps, and rubella vaccine (MMR)
- Meningococcal vaccines
- Pneumococcal vaccine (PCV)

- Polio vaccine (IPV)
- Rotavirus vaccine

*https://www.cdc.gov/vaccines/schedules/index.html

Some vaccines may cause mild reactions, such as soreness where the shot was given or a fever.

But serious reactions are rare. If your child has a serious reaction after a vaccine call your doctor right away or if symptoms are severe then take the child to the emergency room.

Some parents may hesitate to have their kids vaccinated. They may have questions or worry that a child might have a serious reaction or get the illness the vaccine prevents.

But the components of vaccines are weakened or killed. In some cases, only parts of the germ are used. The risk of a serious reaction to a vaccine is minimal compared to the risk of very serious complications from a disease that could have been prevented by a vaccination. It is critical to protect young children by getting them vaccinated because they are more susceptible to diseases since their immune symptoms have not built up yet. By immunizing them by age 2 you will not only help them survive, but also protect those they come in contact with at day care or at school.

A federal program called Vaccines for Children (VCF) allows kids to be vaccinated free of charge. To qualify, they have to be are under the age of 19 and have ONE of the following apply to them--medicaid-eligible, uninsured, underinsured, or American Indian or Alaska Native. Ask your doctor if you are in need of this assistance and how to access it or click on this link: https://www.cdc.gov/vaccines/programs/vfc/index.html

SECTION 3
Back to School Safety

> **SUMMARY**
> 1. Always review safe practices for getting to and from school with your child
> 2. Back to school illnesses are common, especially if you live in an area with high flu risk.
> 3. Keep a safe space in your home for your child to continue learning outside of the classroom.

As summer draws to a close, families and students alike must prepare for the return to school. For children who have never been to preschool or kindergarten, there can be many daunting challenges, such as riding the bus, spotting you in the carline, or contracting an illness.

Not only do teachers need clever classroom management strategies to deal with these problems, but parents also need to make sure their home is a safe place that promotes learning. As a parent you will need to be prepared for new skills being learned by your preschooler who may start becoming more independent and coordinated. A well-organized learning space in the home that has safety procedures in place helps students concentrate on school work and be ready to learn.

At this age, parents can make a game out of having kids learn to pick up their toys so they do not become tripping hazards. They can also learn to store their bicycles and lock outside doors properly.

Some important reminders when crafting such a space include:

1. Keep dangerous objects out of reach

Knives, scissors, bulletin board tacks, and other kitchen utensils should be off limits for preschool-aged kids. Make sure to keep any sharp objects, choking hazards, poisonous materials and other potentially hazardous supplies on a high shelf or locked away in a cupboard.

Lighters and matches should also be put away. Keep cords wound and put away, electrical outlets covered with safety caps and drawers closed and latched especially when not in use.

Magnets can be dangerous if they are small enough to be swallowed as some are on toys.

If supplies are made available during craft time, then children should be supervised and there should be communication about how to safely use these tools.

2. Wash your hands

Hand washing is an easy way to prevent the spread of germs and keep kids safe. When your family is healthy then nobody has to miss work, school or other activities. Regular hand washing is a standard procedure for most classrooms, but it's also one that many preschoolers haven't fully grasped yet, so it's important to reinforce this at home. Set a good example by getting

in the habit of properly washing hands yourself. Make hand washing a typical part of your daily routine. For example, before and after eating, after using the bathroom, after touching pets, after playing outside, and after coughing or sneezing. You can make it entertaining by making up a hand washing song and turning it into another game.

Soap and water are the best way to clean hands. Be sure the water is warm, but not too hot for that delicate preschooler skin. If soap and water is not available, then use an alcohol-based sanitizer with at least 60 percent alcohol. Baby wipes are not made to sanitize hands.

3. Practice emergency plans

Disasters and emergencies can be scary, but if you have prepared your preschooler, then they will better be able to cope with them at home and in school. Remind them that safe practices can keep them safe, before, during and after an emergency. Emergency plans are not as helpful if your preschooler does not know the drill.

Walk kids through the experience before your school's first fire drill. It will help the teacher in charge if the child is in control of his or her emotions. Role play the whole event, from alarm to the moment when it is safe to come back inside.

Then when that first fire drill occurs, your student will not be as afraid.

Do the same thing with lockdown drills, tornado drills and other emergency safety plans.

This will help children understand that their school and teachers take safety seriously.

4. Sanitize everything

Preschoolers are learning sharing skills, but they do not always understand their own private spaces. They share not only toys, but hugs, kisses coughs, and sneezes. It is important to teach your child to not put things in their mouth at home or in school. It may be fun to play with fake vegetables and foods, but putting them in the mouth spreads germs. Clean frequently touched toys and surfaces daily with a regular household detergent and water before disinfecting. How often you clean toys at home depends on how loved they are, but if your child is sick then those toys should be disinfected as soon as they have recovered. Electronic toys can be wiped with a sanitizer, whereas follow washing directions for plush toys which may be able to put in the washing machine. Bath toys and hard plastic toys are the easiest to clean and sanitize though if they are hollow beware of water getting stuck inside which can lead to mold or bacteria growth. Solid plastic toys may be able to carefully be washed in the top rack only of the dishwasher.

5. Beware of Flu Season

The back to school season is further complicated by the beginning of flu season in the United States. Seasonal influenza is often confused with a common cold, though symptoms can differ significantly. The common cold lasts 2-5 days with symptoms like a cough, runny nose, and sore throat. However, with influenza, one also develops fever, chills, muscle aches, headaches, and general weakness and fatigue. Influenza will normally last about one week and will resolve itself. It is recommended that individuals of all ages get the flu vaccine before the season starts unless contraindicated.

Keep in mind that at this age preschoolers cannot understand new risks though they can recognize learn basic rules and recognize when they are not begin followed by self or by others. They may not even remember the rules if they get too excited or are in a complicated situation. And they are not in full control of themselves when asked to slow down. So introducing basic safety rules and following them yourselves as parents and helping your child understand them is of continued importance.

CHAPTER 2

Middle School Development

SECTION 1
Bullying

> **SUMMARY**
> 1. Bullying can have disastrous consequences for everyone involved
> 2. Students, parents, teachers, and the community must all work together to foster a safe, inclusive environment in schools
> 3. Know how to recognize when someone may be the victim of bullying

Bullying is defined by the American Medical Association (AMA) as a pattern of repeated aggression with deliberate intent to harm or disturb a victim despite apparent victim distress and a real or perceived imbalance of power. Bullying can include harassment, gossiping, spreading rumors, threats, or other types of intimidation.

These may be done in person or expand to involve the use of emails, chat rooms, blogs, or social media, which is referred to as cyber-bullying or online bullying.

As your child progresses from elementary school to middle school, the challenges they face on a day to day basis will shift drastically.

Nowhere is this more apparent than within social settings. Although bullying can start as early as preschool, by the time kids reach middle school, it has often become an accepted part of the school. In fact, bullying increases around fifth and sixth grade and continues to get worse until around ninth grade. This is driven by teens' transition into adolescence, and an inner motivation to be accepted by their peers-even if it means putting others down.

Bullying also works as a protective measure for those desperate to fit into a certain social clique. In fact, 30 percent of kids between grades 6 and 10 experience bullying in some form, whether as the agitator or the victim. These estimates are likely even lower than the true percentages, given that over half of all bullying incidents go unreported.

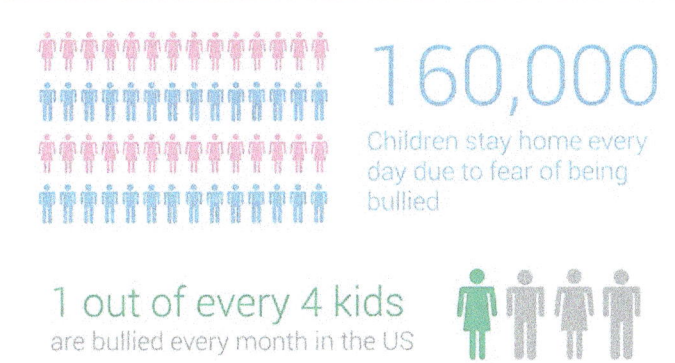

The long and short term effects of bullying are disturbing. Academically, a victim of bullying is likely to do worse than their peers, and will begin to experience "random" health issues, depression, anxiety, difficulty sleeping which may prevent them from attending school. For sustained periods of time, this can lead to complete isolation, lower academic achievement, and dropping out of school. Bullying has a negative effect on how the child feels about themselves, their relationships with friends and family, and their physical health.

Even the bully will likely face problems later in life. Studies have shown that bullies are more likely to display antisocial behavior and violence later in life. Additionally, they are prone to alcohol and drug abuse, and research shows that bul-ies are more likely to commit criminal acts. In fact, bullies are four times more likely than nonbullies to be convicted of crimes by age 24. These statistics show how serious the effects of bullying can be on everyone involved.

Not all unpleasant exchanges between students should be labeled bullying, however. And being left out of parties or gatherings should also not be construed as bullying. Try to ascertain that being bullied is not being used as an excuse for low grades or conflict with other students or something else. Also, at middle school level it is common to see bully-on-bully behavior when name calling or bad behavior occurs from both parties and then one finally seeks the higher authorities. While it is critical to report bullying, it is also very important to develop the coping skills to handle unkind behavior as that is a necessary life skill. Set clear expectations of behavior with your child on how they handle themselves.

So how do you identify when your child, or another, is being bullied?

1. **Signs of Bullying**

    - Fear of going to school or activities or being around certain people
    - Damaged clothing; unexplained cuts/bruises
    - Isolation from friends and family
    - Unprecedented problems at school
    - Academic performance decline
    - Emotional outbursts or crying
    - Sudden onset of medical problems—stomachaches or headaches
    - Sleeping difficulties or loss of appetite
    - Thoughts of suicide

2. Hear your child's story of the bullying incident(s)

It is very important to talk and listen to your child by asking open ended questions.

Tease out the details of the bullying from your child. Be patient and nurturing as they may hesitate in sharing names or be afraid to anger you. Try to be neutral and determine the severity of the problem. Children are concerned that if they tell their parents or talk to the teacher, they will outcast by their peers. They also ask their parents not to intervene by calling the school or the parent of the bully for fear of worse retribution.

Praise the child for telling you and make it clear that bullying is never okay. Reassure them that they are safe. If needed, seek out the authorities at the location, especially if the incident happened at an education site for school, sports or arts.

If cyber bullying is part of the issue, then take photos of the offending screens. Cyber bullying includes things such as hurtful comments, rumors spread online using text, photo or video messaging, social media (for example, Facebook, Twitter, Instagram, Snapchat, YouTube), or cell phones. Carefully monitor your child's social media sites and learn the latest lingo.

3. Coach Your Child on How to React

Practice doing role-play with your child so they know what do or say if someone tries to bully them. Tell them to ignore the bully, walk away, and tell an adult. It is not a good idea to fight back physically or with words. If they react to the bully then they may get picked on further. Bullies choose kids who get upset and who cannot manage being teased, and cannot stand up for themselves.

It is best not to tell the child any of the following: to solve the problem themselves, that bullying wouldn't happen if they acted differently, or to ignore what was going on and do not tattle.

If you feel your child may hurt themselves, seek professional help immediately.

It is imperative that you give positive feedback to your child for appropriate social behaviors and model interactions that do not include bullying or aggression. If possible, work with your child to problem-solve concrete solutions. Teaching peaceful conflict resolution, showing empathy and using good communication skills should be the goal, if possible.

4.   Seek professional resources

It is best not to go directly to the family of the bully to attempt to resolve things as it could become controversial. If the incidents are occurring at school then parents should seek out a school counselor, psychologist or social worker. It is best to establish a positive relationship with the school administration well in advance of any difficulties. They generally only hear from parents when there is a problem so by having a communication line established ahead of time will really help you and your child resolve difficulties.

Control your own feelings and then try to patiently hear the details from your child keeping in mind that there are multiple sides to an event and that the child may not fully reveal everything, especially right away. And when you share these details with the school, control your own emotional intelligence so that you have a productive conversation keeping the goals in mind to ensure the physical and emotional needs of your child.

Collaborate and try to problem solve so that the results are beneficial to all as much as possible. Schools have to manage their legal liabilities as well, but are very committed to manage bullying and making schools a safe place to learn for everyone.

5. Find something your child enjoys

Finding a niche or being a part of something bigger is a way to help your child fit in—a need to belong is something that all of us have. By trying new activities or clubs, your child will meet friends and eventually find something he or she is good at which will help develop self-esteem. This is an important step to eventually prepare for high school as the student body generally gets bigger and there is more to try and do at that stage, but also many more students with whom to interact

SECTION 2
Social Media and MentalHealth

> **SUMMARY**
> 1. Talk to your child about proper online conduct
> 2. Set limits on video games and entertainment websites
> 3. Stay in the know on the current popular apps with your child and their friends

It is no surprise to anyone that the use of social media has increased dramatically among teens over the last few years. This form of media offer teens a portal for socialization and entertainment. Exposure begins early in life for many youth, with those under age two having almost three-fourths of an hour of screen time. By the time they reach middle school, computers, smartphones and social media are a fully immersive experience. In some schools tablets or laptops are issued to each student to manage the online curriculum.

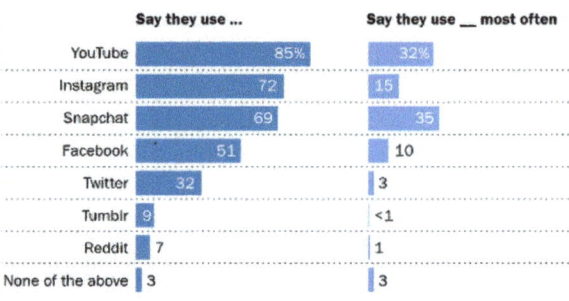

As early as age 11, young people can expect to have access to smart phones. According to the Pew Research Center, most middle and high school age youth have access to a computer (88 percent) at home. Computer access varies by family income and education level. However, nearly all teens age 13-17 (95 percent) own a smart-phone. Most teens (84 percent), especially boys (92 percent) own or have access to game consoles. These devices can be used not only to call or text, but also to play games and access the Internet, including a rapidly expanding number of social media sites.

It is important for parents to be familiar with the types of social media sites given that not all are healthy for growing teens. Broadly defined, social media is any digital application that allows people to interact socially. It may include social networking sites like Instagram, Snapchat, Facebook, TikTok, text messaging and messaging apps, social gaming tools, YouTube, and much more. Understanding of your teen's mental health requires careful consideration of the role of social media. This age group is at a higher risk for the onset mental illness with depression, eating disorders, and suicide rates increasing significantly in the last few years. Rapid development of the brain's social core lends itself to greater sensitivity on the social scale. This means that teens are more concerned about approval from their peers.

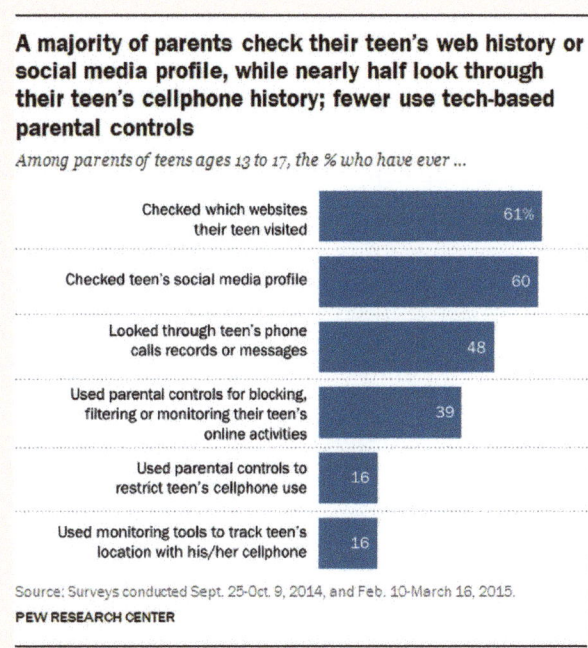

Cyberbullying has run rampant over the past decade as access to technology and the internet has become more widespread. One common app among teens, Snapchat, automatically deletes messages after they have been viewed by the recipient, opening the door for hurtful behavior due to a lack of evidence for repercussions. Other apps, like Youtube or Tik Tok, are more focused on entertainment than communication, but still see their fair share of bullying. With peers being available constantly online, personal information being displayed publicly with comments for all to see, the constant quantifiable "likes" for posts, there is increasing pressure on teens to "perform" or "be on" at all times. They are in the mode of "FOMO" (fear of missing out) and become distracted from their duties or school work.

At a younger age, it can be beneficial to help teach children how to safely use social media to avoid mistakes later on. By setting guidelines on when to use social media, how to use it and where to use it and keeping the communication open around the topic, you will help your teen learn to maneuver what is new and different terrain for everyone.

How parents decide to set and enforce rules for social media usage and monitor internet usage, can vary greatly, and there is no one right

Section 3
Preparing for High School

> **SUMMARY**
> 1. Find your niche
> 2. Try new opportunities
> 3. Get organized
> 4. Think about the future
> 5. Use your support system

Moving from middle school to high school is an exciting time for students and parents. Parents work together with their child and teachers to ensure that there is a successful transition.

Middle schoolers who attend high quality school programs are more likely to show progress by grade level, are more socially competent, and have a better understanding of verbal and math concepts

National graduation rates average in the United States is about 88 percent, with the average state graduation rates of 74-94 percent in the 2017-2018 academic year per the data reported by over 17,000 ranked schools in the 2020 U.S. News Best High Schools rankings (**XX**). These rates help determine how well a high school is serving its students (it is the proportion of students who started in ninth grade and graduated four years later).

In high school, classes start to get significantly more difficult as teachers try to prepare students for college. Students also have the opportunity to do things that you could never do in middle school like driving to school and attending Homecoming and Prom.

However, the transition from middle school to high school can raise concerns for both your child and you. Instead of being the oldest students around, 8th graders find that as freshmen, they are the youngest in the building. Acclimating to a new building or high school campus, understanding teachers' expectations, a bigger workload, fitting in socially and making new friends, are just some of the  things your child may worry about. You may be more concerned with the school work load and time management, proper selection of classes that are the best fit, getting safely to and from school, peer pressures, and how to help your student seek any additional resources needed.

Therefore, how can you best prepare your child for high school?

1.   Attend high school orientation

While this may be time consuming and your child may be resistant to go, it is very important to attend high school orientation or open house if it is offered. If it is not, then contact the school at the end of the school year or a few days prior to the school opening for your child's freshman year and ask for a tour. Seeing

the building, walking through the hallways, and knowing where some of the main rooms like the library, cafeteria, bathrooms, gymnasium, front office, and nurse's office are may bring comfort to your freshman.

Schools share their policies for dress code, cell phone usage, early and late arrival, whether it is an open campus at lunch, and general expectations during these events.

2. Practice getting to school

Regardless of how your student plans to get to school, practice getting there a few times. Follow the route in your car (even if they will be riding the school bus), and show them where to get on and off the bus. If they will be walking or biking, then follow the path and determine where to lock the bicycle and what door to enter from at the school. It is also a good idea to have certain places called out as safe zones (a business or a familiar house on the path) in case your student needs help. Going to school with a friend is generally a good idea and safer. It may also provide more comfort for you as a parent knowing your child is not alone.

3. Good study routine and homework review

While it may be easy to spread out at the dining table, a separate area is more conducive to good study habits and better concentration. Help your child keep a log of assignments in one place since some of their work may be online and some on paper. Review those assignments along with extracurricular activities and tests with your student weekly. If you establish this routine, over time they will be able to

work independently ad do it themselves. This will help them prioritize and maybe even complete projects ahead of time to juggle workload and be more efficient.

Reviewing class notes or previous assignments before starting homework also helps with memory retention so that at the time of the test they are more familiar with the content. If possible, have them start with the most difficult assignments first while they are fresh.

4. Course selection

Some schools offer tests in middle school to determine student levels for highs school courses. Class levels most suited to your student are suggested by the teachers, but parents also play a role in the final selection. It is best to allow your child to be put into their comfortable pace of learning instead of pushing them to do more. There are enough pressures on them with a new school environment and changing bodies, without signing up for courses that may not allow them reach their full potential.

5. Teach accountability/independent learning

Encourage your middle schooler towards more independence by having them begin to do a variety of things for themselves if they have not done so already. Tasks such as setting their own morning alarm, making their own lunches, creating their own schedules and doing their chores without being asked will all lead to more self-directed learning. Even homework schedule review should be done weekly and then give them more latitude to manage it themselves with periodic check-ins. Have consequences for incomplete tasks as that is best for behavioral change, especially when the student has been made aware of the expectations.

6. Self care and mindfulness

Talk to your child about their changing bodies and the need for better self-care. High school brings about numerous challenges so having a workout routine, or finding ways to relax and be with family and friends and making healthy choices is very important. Being mindful of the tasks at hand and working through them one step at a time can help from becoming overwhelmed.

7. School supplies on hand

Schools generally provide a school supply list so review that and allow time to buy the supplies well in advance, as back to school sales sometimes cause a temporary shortage of certain items.

8. Review 8th grade material in summer

Children who do not review school materials over the summer fall behind on average of three months in reading and two months in math (**XX**). Much of the knowledge that students gained in the school year gets forgotten, and teachers spend precious class time "re-teaching" concepts from the previous year. Even a minimum of thirty minutes of reading a day will help your student retain some of the knowledge they already learned so the transition back to class in September is an easier one. Reading current events can also help them be familiar with world issues around them and they will have some topics to share at the dinner table.

9. Select extracurricular activities wisely

Middle school can be used to explore outside activities that your student can build upon in highschool. In high school they can follow this activity with passion and determination as that is what colleges like to see. Encourage your child to sign up for clubs and explore different interests.

10. Open communication

As teens grow and seek more independence, conflict arises. They still yearn for parental approval though even if they seem more distant andfilled with rebellion. On an emotional level, as a parent you need to set boundaries and follow

CHAPTER 3

High School Development

Section 1
Drug Abuse

> **SUMMARY**
> 1. Talk to your child and develop a plan for avoiding drugs
> 2. Address underlying issues and encourage honesty
> 3. Be informed about signs of drug abuse
> 4. Get help when necessary

More than 42,500 students from nearly 400 public and private schools across the country participated in "Monitoring the Future (MTF)", a survey of drug use and attitudes among American 8th, 10th, and 12th graders. Trends continue to be seen for cigarette use, with past month use down by approximately 20-30 percent compared to the mid-1990's. Declines were seen in five-year trends of lifetime, past year, past month and binge alcohol use and in overall rates of lifetime, past year and past month illicit drug use, excluding marijuana, among 10th and 12th graders. No tably, misuse of prescription opioids among high school seniors is at

its lowest rate since the survey began assessing it. Despite these positive trends, the 2019 MTF results show a continued dramatic increase in vaping.

Additionally, substance use by teens can have a significant impact on their health and well-being. The American Academy of Pediatrics (AAP), through an agreement with the Center for Disease Control and Prevention (CDC), developed a guide for implementing substance use screening in pediatric practices to help pediatricians address substance use concerns. They highlighted the following key points:

- Alcohol, marijuana, and tobacco are substances most commonly used and abused drugs by high schoolers that can cause these problems include:
- Cocaine — Risk of heart attack, stroke and seizures
- Ecstasy — Risk of liver failure and heart failure
- Inhalants — Risk of damage to heart, lungs, liver and kidneys from long-term use
- Marijuana — Risk of impairment in memory, learning, problem solving and concentration; risk of psychosis — such as schizophrenia, hallucination or paranoia — later in life associated with early and frequent use
- Methamphetamine — Risk of psychotic behaviors from long-term use or high doses
- Opioids — Risk of respiratory distress or death from overdose
- Electronic cigarettes (vaping) — Exposure to harmful substances similar to exposure from cigarette smoking; risk of nicotine dependence

With such high stakes, many teachers, administrators, and parents are right to be worried about the activities students may choose to do in their free time.

Parents must be prepared to tackle drug and alcohol abuse issues head-on by identifying the often underlying issue at stake.

Some of the most common reasons that high school seniors reported they vape, smoke, or do drugs are to, "experiment", "because it tastes good", "to have a good time with my friends", and "to relax or relieve tension." But in reality, studies from the Mayo Clinic have shown that background and family issues have a greater impact on drug use than any other factor. So how can you show your child how to have a good time without illicit substances?

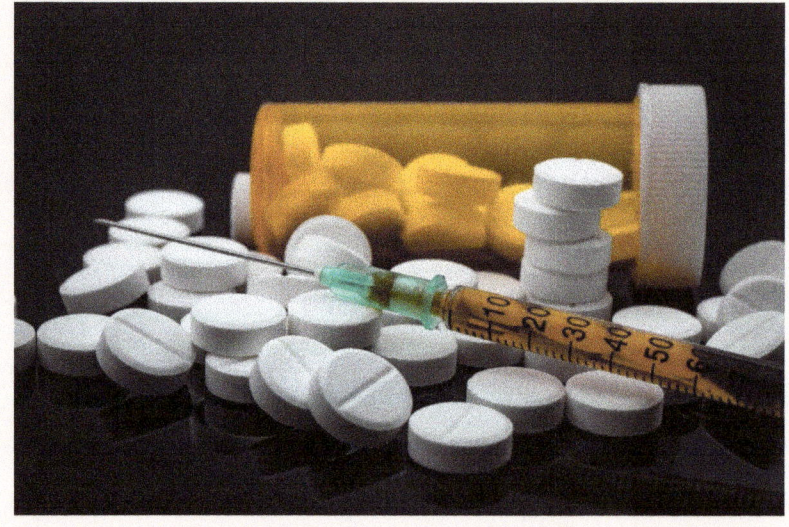

Talk to them. Ask your child what their views on, and avoid lecturing. Assure your child that honesty will always be rewarded. In addition, discuss ways to avoid drugs or to not be the victim of peer pressure. Brainstorm how to turn down offers and to extricate themselves from a dangerous situation.

Some other productive strategies provided by the Mayo Clinic include:

- Knowing your teen's activities. Pay attention to your teen's whereabouts. Find out what adult-supervised activities your teen is interested in and encourage him or her to get involved.

- Establishing rules and consequences. Explain your family rules, such as leaving a party where drug use occurs and not riding in a car with a driver who's been using drugs. If your teen breaks the rules, consistently enforce consequences.
- Knowing your teen's friends. If your teen's friends use drugs, your teen might feel pressure to experiment, too.
- Keeping track of prescription drugs. Take an inventory of all prescription and over-the-counter medications in your home.
- Providing support. Offer praise and encouragement when your teen succeeds. A strong bond between you and your teen might help prevent your teen from using drugs.
- Setting a good example. If you drink, do so in moderation. Use prescription drugs as directed. Don't use illicit drugs.

Section 2
Recognizing and Treating Mental Health Issues

> **SUMMARY**
> 1. Be ready to identify signs of mental health
> 2. Create a support structure for those around you
> 3. Know the resources at your disposal for dealing with minor or major mental health issues

Stress is one of the most prevalent causes of mental health issues. It has been shown to causeanxiety attacks, major depression, minor depression, drug abuse, mental illness, and violent behaviors, such as suicide or self-harm.

Students of all age groups can exhibit the symptoms of stress, but during the high school and college years it is more often an issue. Social isolation, strong emotional reactions, and erratic behavior have all been linked to stress. Often times it is difficult to identify the cause of the stress since different circumstances can spark different reactions in students.

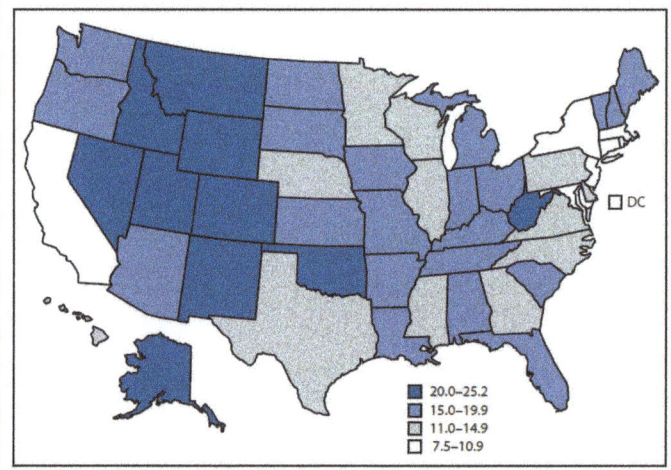

According to the APA, "Stress can be a short-term reaction in response to an upcoming event, such as speaking in front of the class. Stress can also result from ongoing experiences, such as coping with parents' divorce or adapting to different cultural or social expectations or values. Some

amount of stress is beneficial and can motivate students to perform better. Too much stress can be harmful, even if it is associated with sowing the seeds for a positive event (e.g., academic/ sports competition or going to college)".

When stress gets out of control, it can cause self-harm or even suicide. Compared to the rest of the nation, Michigan was ranked 23rd for the highest rate of mental illness, with the most common being depression. In Michigan, an alarming trend of suicide is going, with some estimates from the CDC and NPR reporting an increase of 33%. Another condition, Seasonal Affe tive Disorder (SAD), is common, especially in the long Michigan winters. This causes some to become depressed in the winter months. Common over the counter remedies for SAD includes Cardamom, which detoxifies the body and rejuvenates cells, nutmeg, which stimulates the brain and relieves fatigue, saffron, which increases serotonin, honey, which relaxes frayed nerves, and apples, which can help repair brain nerve cells. Foods high in vitamin B6, such as chicken, have been shown to have an impact on serotonin, which may help alleviate the symptoms of SAD.

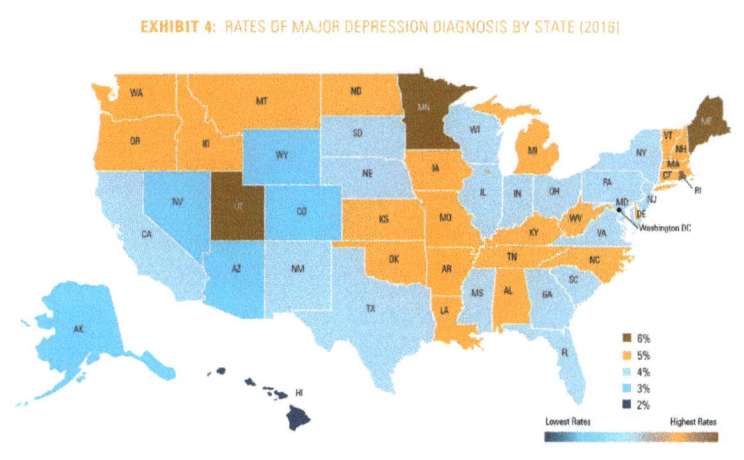

EXHIBIT 4: RATES OF MAJOR DEPRESSION DIAGNOSIS BY STATE (2016)

Suicide is a taboo topic which many feel uncomfortable talking about. However, it must be acknowledged before we can begin to combat this issue. Suicide is the tenth leading cause of death in the United States, and it is the second leading cause between ages fifteen and thirty four, second only to unintentional injuries. About 123 Americans take their lives everyday, which averages one every 12.3 seconds. Globally, 800,000 people take their own lives each year. Most suicides occur in middle and low income countries, predominantly in Europe and Africa, but we cannot ignore even a single death.

Many contribute suicide to mental illness, medical issues, PTSD, social isolation, and family conflict. These can also contribute to self harm. Self harm is another taboo topic, however it is much less publicized and known about compared to suicide. In 2017, the latest available data, 494,169 people visited a hospital for self harm behavior. This means about approximately 12 people harm themselves for every 1 person who commits suicide.

To help reduce suicide and alleviate stress among high school students, it is imperative to implement a support structure. This burden lies among parents, teachers, and even a student's peers. Some common strategies include:

1. Express explicit concern and offer help
2. Offer ways to cope, such as creating a safe space
3. Speak about concerning behavior privately so as not to embarrass them
4. Review school policy about working with therapists, counselors, or psychologists
5. Reach out to a professional if there is any risk of self-harm or suicide

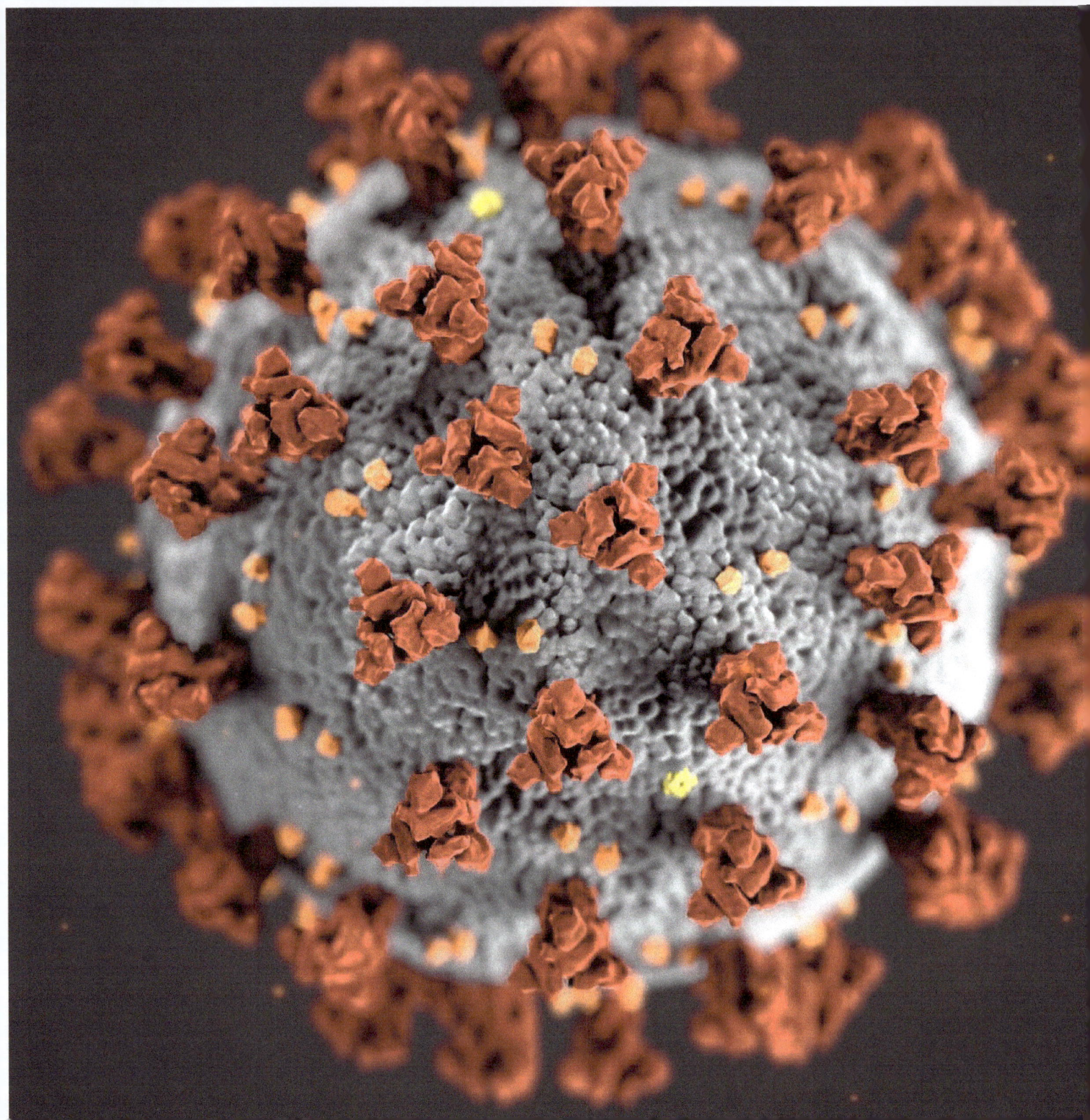

CHAPTER 4

COVID-19 and Development

SECTION 1
The Impact of Social Distancing on Children

> **SUMMARY**
> 1. Help keep children healthy
> 2. Create and enforce a daily routine to create normalcy
> 3. Help children connect socially in distanced and COVID-conscious ways
> 4. Recognize and address fear and stress
> 5. Be a good role model

The year 2020 will always be remembered as the most widespread and deadly pandemic in recent memory. Covid-19, which first appeared in December of 2019, reshaped society and drastically changed the world as we know it. The World Health Organization declared COVID-19 to be a full-scale pandemic in March of 2020. Soon after, schools, businesses, and restaurants followed suit, effectively bringing life to standstill.

Between its discovery and December of 2020, there have been 74 million recorded cases of COVID-19 internationally, resulting in an estimated 1.7 million deaths. At the time of publication of this book, the curve representing new cases is still rising, along with the death count.

While several vaccines have been developed and approved to prevent transmission of the virus, a clear cure for those infected has not yet been found. As a result, to prevent transmission, strict stay-at-home orders, mask mandates, and limitations on gatherings exist.

In addition to these everyday steps to prevent COVID-19, physical or social distancing is one of the best tools we have to avoid being exposed to the virus and to slow its spread. However, this can have myriad adverse effects on children's' development.

When children are very young, their parents and caregivers— including extended family members, a worship community, and childcare workers— provide them with daily caretaking routines that support their development and well-being. Disruptions in these routines and the sudden loss of usual caregivers due to the need to physically distance can be traumatic for young children. 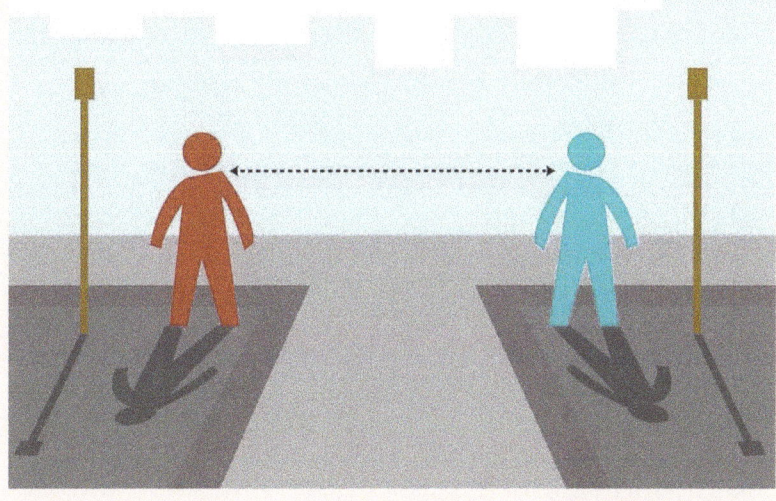 It is important for parents to support young children by ensuring their own social, emotional, and mental health. Establishing routines and structure for young children with other trusted caregivers who also practice social distancing and hygiene measures can provide support to parents with caretaking responsibilities, giving parents time to take healthy steps to cope with their own stress.

For adolescents and older children, missed events can cause greater problems than breaks in routine. Birthdays, graduations, talent shows, vacation plans, births, and funerals are just a sample of the many significant life events that children may have missed experiencing during COVID-19. Social distancing, stay-at-home orders, and limits to gatherings have affected the ability of friends and family to come together in person to celebrate or grieve in typical ways. It is important to help children understand that hosting gatherings during COVID-19 could be dangerous to those who would want to participate. Family and friends can help them find alternate ways to connect and support each other at a distance, such as Zoom or Facetime calls.

Long periods without extra-familial interactions have proven to be extremely harmful for the psychological health of older children as well. The full extent of these impact on minors remains to be seen, but so far, researchers have concluded that it can change drastically based on several key factors. Among these are developmental age, the presence of underlying medical/psychological conditions, or economic privilege. As a result, children may develop feelings of sadness or anxiety that can last for months.

Additionally, since schools are enclosed spaces with large groups of people and often out-of-date of dysfunctional ventilation systems, the majority of teaching has occurred over the internet. Services such as Zoom or Slack give teachers the opportunity to see and virtually interact with their students in a pseudo-classroom setting, without incurring the risk of viral transmission. However, this can be a poor substitute for physical contact.

To help safely and swiftly address these problems without violating distancing guidelines requires careful attention by school administrators, parents, and peers. Below are some strategies for doing so, as proposed by the CDC.

1.   Help keep children healthy

Schedule wellness and immunization visits for children. Seek continuity in mental and occupational health care. Help children to eat healthy and drink water – instead of sugar sweetened beverages – for strong teeth. Encourage children to play outdoors— it's great for physical and men tal health, and can help children stay healthy and focused.

2. Help children stay socially connected

Reach out to friends and family via phone or video chats. Write cards or letters to family members they may not be able to visit. Schools may have tips and guidelines to help support social and emotional needs of children.

3. Recognize and address fear and stress

Adolescence is a time of big changes. Adolescents can be particularly overwhelmed when stress is related to a traumatic event, expressed as excessive worry or sadness, unhealthy eating or sleeping habits, and difficulty with attention and concentration. Adults can provide stability and support to help them cope, as well as facilitate access to professional help and distress emergency hotlines, as needed.

4. Help young adults take care of themselves and their community

Taking care of friends and family can be a stress reliever, but it should be balanced with self-care. Young adults can help make their community stronger by helping others cope with their stress, such as by providing social support, and following everyday actions to prevent getting sick and slow the spread of COVID-19. Being a good role model is key—if young adults wash their hands often, stay at least 6 feet apart from others, and wear their masks in public spaces to help protect themselves and others, then their peers are more likely to do the same.

The Physical and Mental Health Impact on Children during Covid-19 pandemic.

The year 2020 will always be remembered as the world's most widespread and deadly pandemic. The World Health Organization (WHO) declared Covid-19 a pandemic in March 2020, and soon afterward all schools, restaurants, hotels, and local businesses closed as an effort to suppress the virus.

Here we are, almost 17 months later, and we are still unable to control the infections by Covid-19 and the variants due to mutation of the virus. We also have emerging strains of the viruses that are affecting our children and seniors. In the United States, as reported by current CDC protocol, as of last month American children were being affected more due to transmission of sars-cov-2 virus. It is hard to predict how the data will look since it is changing every day.

Here is what we have learnt so far:

The symptoms of Covid-19-sars include fever, fatigue, headaches, myalgia, coughing, sneezing and more non-specific symptoms like flu or seasonal allergies. Current evidence according to CDC and WHO suggest that children with underlying illnesses such as diabetes, hypertension, and chronic asthma suffer more and more and need hospitalizations.

Testing, isolation, and quarantine for our school-aged children.

What are the criteria's for testing?

Above mentioned signs and symptoms, plus close contact with someone with lab confirmed Covid-19.

High likelihood for exposure such as living in a closed community, travelling, participating in closed sports activity, or very active with social media.

Our health care workers should work with families to keep updated with childhood immunizations, necessary vaccines and upcoming influenza vaccine for early fall.

What are the recent guidelines for vaccination of kids and teenagers?

www.childrenshospital.org corona vaccines

Can children get vaccines? The clinical trials for Covid-19 vaccines above 12 years of age have been approved. After several studies done by the world health organization. In collaboration with FDA and CDC to recommend the vaccines in kids above 12 years of age.

What are the clinical symptoms of depression in children during pandemic?

Look around at the children around you, some of them might be struggling with mental issues.

The factual statistics from the National Institute of Mental Health reveals that probably 1 in 5 children all over the United States are affected by this serious, debilitating mental illness. However, statistics have revealed that most of them recover completely with early diagnosis and treatment. But the major barrier to this stigma is the aura and fear due to loss of their family members, friends, loss of job, financial issues, away from their friends at school and more.

What are the physical impacts of a pandemic?

Malnutrition due to under feeding, obesity due to inadequate proper nutritious food, hx of underlined diseases such as diabetes, hypertension, improper behaviours and more.

Although medical literatures initially showed that children were minimally susceptible to 2019 Covid-19. THE CURRENT EVIDENCE SHOWS THAT CHILDRENS ARE THE VICTIMS OF COVID 19 VARIANT SO CALLED DELTA VARIANT. They are hit hardest by psycho social impact from the pandemic. The full impact of quarantine, social isolation from their friends, missing school lunches, loss of job of their parents or caretakers, death of family members all TOGETHER HAVE BROUGHT A significant impact on children .

WHAT ARE THE ROLE OF PARENTS, CARETAKERS, SCHOOL ADVISORS AND MENTAL HEALTH STAFFS?

1. Open communication with your child, their pediatrician, connect with other families and work out with school systems.

2. Many students across the nation are dealing with sudden changes to their social lives and daily routines, inability to access proper food and nutrition due to financial insecurity, inability to attend schools, social isolations and more. These challenges can present with feelings of sadness and anxiety and stress among children.

3. Parents struggling with their own life, have problems balancing the family life with their professional career and need help themselves towards raising their children during the crisis.

What have we learnt so far regarding Covid-19 vaccine and its variant for children's vaccination during pandemic? The important vaccines manufacturing are Pfizer,

Moderna and Johnsons. Since this is a global pandemic the pharmaceutical companies all over the world are experimenting with new vaccines. The most pertinent one is the Pfizer vaccine administered in 2 doses 4 weeks apart.

WHAT DO WE KNOW ABOUT THE NEW VARIANT OF COVID 19?

The delta variant of coronavirus with k417n mutation was first reported in India however later on similar cases were reported from South Africa, Europe and other countries from where several mutants have been isolated. These mutants are affecting our children getting sick due to being highly transmitted through contacts.

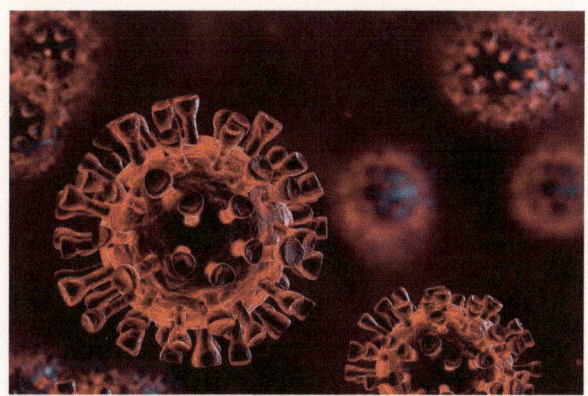

What is delta plus?

It is a sub lineage of delta variant 1st detected in India being carried by bats in mountain caves and has acquired the spike protein mutation k417 which is also found in the Beta variant 1st identified in south Africa. AS reported by top virologists in India this variant reduces the effectiveness of a cocktail of therapeutic monoclonal antibodies.

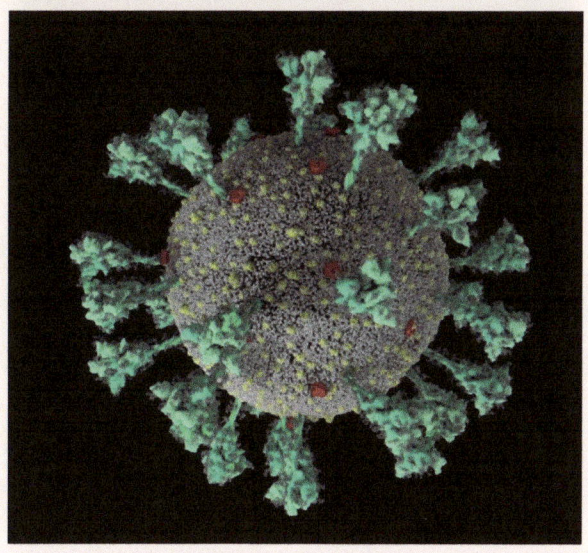

As of June 16, 2021 at least 197 cases have been reported in 11 countries: Britain, Canada, Nepal, Russia, Switzerland, Turkey, Japan, India and the United states.

What are our concerns?

According to WHO, CDC, American Academy of Pediatrics, many experiments are being done in scientific labs all over the world to control the emergence of this virus and protect our children. Much information regarding this variant is available at the websites mentioned below.

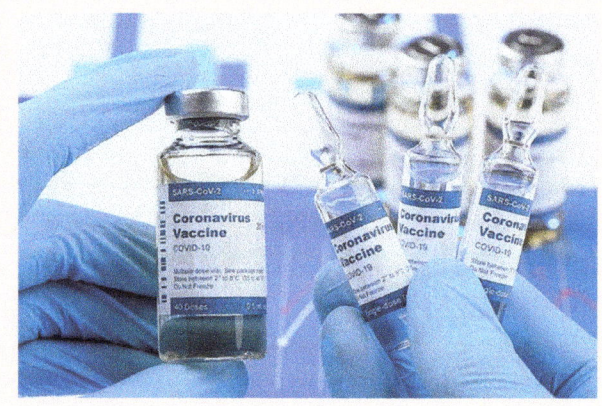

How to keep our children and adolescents safe during the Covid-19 and delta variants?

A proper immunization to all our children including the flu vaccines, as well vaccines against the Covid-19 sars. Maintain social distance, wear masks as needed,

Personal cleanliness, proper nutrition of our children and frequent check up by their pediatrician and mental health specialist.

The Delta variant carries the genetic code from two other mutations E484Q and l452R hence it becomes easy to break into the human immune system. The new variants change the structure of protein hence attaches to the human host cell and multiplies causing more damage. This is highly virulent and attacks the vaccinated as well as non-vaccinated individuals however the vaccinated individual's symptoms are less and that is why mass vaccinations are advised .

Recent published article from Yale medicine.org updated as of July 27, 2021 has described the significant character of Delta D virus.

The world health organization in collaboration with CDC and FDA has classified this virus as the fastest variant of concern. Recent study from United Kingdom showed that children and adults under 50 are more susceptible to this.

The Delta could lead to hyper local outbreaks as reported from US and UK the delta plus has one additional mutation called k417n that affects the spike protein that the virus needs to infect cells and that is the main target aimed at while vaccines are prepared to target the viruses and help produce antibodies in blood to fight infection. Symptoms of disease and other vaccines.

Following are the bibliography and acknowledgement of references mentioned in my book.

1. The American Academy of Pediatrics www.aap.org,
2. CDC www.cdc.gov,
3. WHO www.who.int,
4. www.who.int Health Topics.
5. medscape cme.co
6. ACP The American College of Physician webacponline.org.
7. The National Institute of Drug Abuse.www.drugabuse.gov,
8. TOP Mental Health News in Children. www.healthhealthcareknow.com,
9. Pediatrics weekly highlights from JAMA network web updates@ jamanetwork.com,

10. Chris Shreve web drchrisallenshreve.com.
11. Children's Hospital of Philadelphia web www.chop.edu.

Conclusion

When constructing a skyscraper, if one were to ask the lead engineers about the most critical phase that requires the highest degree of care, precision, and accuracy, they would invariably state that the foundation is most imperative for the entire structure's integrity. Foundations of buildings typically consist of many piles and reinforcing materials driven deep into the ground, oftentimes many stories below the first floor of the structure itself. As such, while the upper floors of buildings require aesthetic finishes, architectural designs, and overall pleasurable appearances, the foundation is but completely invisible. No one cares about the texture or tone of the reinforcing beams, or the blocks of concrete, that lie deep below the surface.

Yet if one were to question the nature of the foundation—its structural traits such as strength, torsional integrity, shear, resistance to temperature change or moisture—then suddenly everyone in the building (especially those on the upper floors!) would care. They would become anxious, and question the strength of the building. They would wonder if the building might catastrophically fail if some external pressure were applied to it. It is unlikely that any of the building's occupants would know even the slightest bit of information about skyscraper construction, or building foundations—however, they would certainly attest to the importance of careful attention paid to the construction process such that the final product was highly successful. Regardless of how the foundation was crafted and placed, and regardless of how the skyscraper was built, it must be done well: for everyone's sake.

The topics covered in this book are the foundation to any healthy child's skyscraper of life. As life progresses and one moves from childhood to adolescence, high school to college, training to the working world, and retirement to passing on, each individual in this world slowly ascends their skyscraper, adding floors and floors of experiences until one is quite wise and weathered.

However, as always, the foundation remains the most critical aspect of the structure. The Burj Khalifa can only tower over Dubai without simply collapsing in the wind due to the integrity of its foundation. All future life experiences, all subsequent floors—everything is dependent on the quality of early life parenting and guidance, ensuring that children follow positive paths while ignoring perilous ones.

Further, many foundations are constructed in different ways—there is no "one" path to raise a child, or one mechanism that is "correct" or "incorrect." All foundations have the potential to be strong and integral. However, if certain building blocks and essential checklist items are attended to during the critical shaping years of adolescence, foundations are much more likely to breed success in the long term. Thus, in this book I have strived to provide you as many of these building block as I can based on my decades of experience in the field. I hope that you choose to apply some, disregard some, and generally combine my advice with your own perspective and value structure when making decisions about how to best guide your children into a beautiful future filled with green.

My book is geared towards parents, caretakers, grandparents and our children, about how to raise a healthy child and how to prevent injuries, accidents, and drug use.

Being a pediatrician and emergency medicine physician with widespread clinical knowledge, as well having raised my own family with, including 4 children and 8 grandchildren, I have learned a lot.

The outline of my book focuses upon 3 groups of children: ages 2 to 5; 5 to 12; and 12 to 18. While it is very hard to cover all the problems as well as diseases encountered in children, I chose to discuss the most encountered health issues and burning topics among children at home and at school.

My emphasis is towards their good health, nutrition and preventative measures from accidents, injuries, bad habits and more. These are my own ideas and suggestions.

Lastly, I have always encouraged our readers to keep in touch with their own primary care physicians and follow their advice.